RASPBERRY FARMING

From Seedling To Harvest, Learn The Basic Process Of Growing Raspberries.

Dr. Smith M. Lama

Copyright © 2024 by Dr. Smith M. Lama

All rights reserved. No part of this publication may be reproduced, distributed, or transmitted in any form or by any means, including photocopying, recording, or other electronic or mechanical methods, without the prior written permission of the publisher, except in the case of brief quotations embodied in critical reviews and certain other noncommercial uses permitted by copyright law.

Disclaimer:

The information provided on this page is intended for general informational purposes only and should not be construed as professional advice. While every effort has been made to ensure the accuracy and completeness of the content, we make no representations or warranties of any kind, express or implied, about the reliability, suitability, or availability of the information contained herein.

Readers are advised to consult with qualified professionals or experts in the relevant field for specific guidance or advice tailored to their individual needs and circumstances. The authors, publishers, and contributors of this book shall not be held liable for any loss, damage, or inconvenience arising from the use of or reliance on the information presented in this publication.

Contents

Overview of Raspberry Farming 6

CHAPTER ONE 9

The Origins And History Of Raspberries 9
Health Advantages 12
Adverse Reactions 15
Useful parts 18
Chemical constituents 21

CHAPTER TWO 25

Varieties, Along With Information On Their Habitat And Cultivation Methods. 25
Propagation 32
The right planting season 42
Planting techniques, depths, and spacing 46
Methods for preserving and storing 50

CHAPTER THREE 54

Weed Control 54
How To Control Pests And Diseases 59
Chemical Fertilizers, Irrigation Techniques, And Fertilizing.. 65

[4]

Methods For Pruning 70

Harvesting And Handling After Harvesting. 76

Handling After Harvest: 78

How To Promote And Make Sales From Raspberry Farming. 81

Overview of Raspberry Farming

Gardening raspberry plants for the purpose of producing raspberries, a well-liked and healthful fruit with a distinct sweet-tart taste, is known as raspberry farming, often referred to as raspberry cultivation or raspberry gardening. Raspberries are members of the rose family and are highly desirable for their intense colors, smooth texture, and plenty of antioxidants.

Growing raspberries entails planting and tending to the plants, which are usually planted in rows on trellises or other supports to enhance air circulation and make picking easier. Raising fruit on canes in their second year, raspberries are perennial plants that need frequent pruning and upkeep to maximize fruit yield.

Among the techniques used in raspberry farming are soil preparation, irrigation, fertilization, control of pests and diseases, pruning, and harvesting. Raspberries are appropriate for cultivation in a variety of climates and places because they grow well in well-drained soil that receives enough sunshine and water.

Due to the market's strong demand for both fresh raspberries and processed goods like jams, jellies, and desserts, raspberry farming is a lucrative endeavor for growers. Thanks to their many culinary uses and health advantages, raspberries are a favorite fruit among consumers.

Raspberry producers can boost the yield and caliber of their products by embracing sustainable farming methods, making use of contemporary technologies, and putting in place quality control procedures.

Furthermore, pick-your-own farms and farm-to-table experiences, as well as value-added product development, are made possible by raspberry cultivation.

CHAPTER ONE

The Origins And History Of Raspberries

Rubus idaeus, the scientific name for raspberries, has a captivating genesis story and a long history. The following are important facts about the origins and history of raspberries:

Origins:

Eastern Asia, namely China, Japan, and Korea, is said to be the birthplace of raspberries.

Wild raspberries have also been discovered to grow around the world, including in North America and Europe.

Ancient times:

Raspberries have been cultivated and consumed for a very long time—back to ancient times.

Raspberries were known to have been farmed and cherished by the Greeks and Romans for their taste and therapeutic qualities.

Cultural Importance:

Raspberries were connected to a number of myths and tales in European folklore. In several cultures, raspberries were associated with love, fertility, and protection.

Medical Applications:

Traditional medicine used raspberries to cure sore throats, inflammation, and digestive problems, among other purported health advantages.

Herbal teas and tonics were also made from the leaves of the raspberry plant.

Gardening:

In Europe during the middle Ages, raspberries were grown in gardens and monasteries. Over time, raspberry farming extended to other regions of the world, including North America.

Present Day Farming:

Raspberries were first grown commercially in the 18th and 19th centuries, when superior kinds were created for increased taste and yield.

Raspberries are now cultivated all over the world, with Serbia, Poland, Russia, and the United States being the main producers.

Health Advantages

In addition to being tasty, raspberries are loaded with nutrients that have a host of health advantages. The following are a few of raspberries' main health advantages:

- Ellagic acid, quercetin, and vitamin C are just a few of the antioxidants that can be found in raspberries. By defending the body against oxidative stress and inflammation, these antioxidants lower the chance of developing chronic illnesses.
- The abundance of antioxidants, potassium, and fiber in raspberries helps promote heart health. Potassium helps control blood pressure, which lowers the risk of heart disease, while fiber helps decrease cholesterol levels.
- By promoting the development of white blood cells and strengthening the body's

resistance to infections and diseases, the vitamin C in raspberries helps strengthen the immune system.
- Heart disease, diabetes, and cancer are just a few of the chronic illnesses that are associated with inflammation in the body, which can be lessened by the phytonutrients in raspberries.
- High in dietary fiber, raspberries aid in a healthy digestive system and help ward against constipation. In addition, fiber promotes the formation of gut flora, which is essential to gut health in general.
- Packed in fiber and minimal in calories, raspberries are an excellent choice for managing weight. The fiber content lowers the chance of overeating by keeping you feeling full and comfortable.
- By shielding the skin from harm brought on by free radicals, raspberries'

antioxidants may help maintain healthy skin and lessen the appearance of aging.

- By delaying the rate at which sugar enters the system, raspberries' high fiber content can assist with controlling blood sugar levels. For people who already have diabetes or are at risk of getting it, this can be helpful.

Adverse Reactions

Even though raspberries have many health advantages, it's vital to be aware of any possible negative effects, particularly for those who may be allergic to or sensitive to raspberries. The following are some possible adverse consequences of eating raspberries:

- Some people may have an allergy to raspberries, which may cause symptoms including breathing difficulties, swelling, itching, or rashes. Get medical help right away if you have any allergic reactions after eating raspberries.
- Due to their high fiber content, raspberries may cause bloating, gas, or diarrhea in some people, particularly if ingested in excessive amounts. To give your digestive system time to adapt, it's

essential to progressively moderate your consumption of meals high in fiber.

- If ingested in excess, pesticide residues from traditionally produced raspberries can be hazardous to health. If you want to reduce your exposure to pesticides, think about buying organic raspberries or properly cleaning them before eating.
- Compounds in raspberries have the ability to interact with several drugs. Before ingesting a lot of raspberries, speak with your doctor if you are on any drugs for blood pressure, diabetes, or blood clotting issues.
- Oxalates, which are present in a lot of fruits and vegetables, can trigger kidney stones in those who are vulnerable. Raspberries are no exception. Reduce the amount of foods rich in oxalate, such as raspberries, if you have a history of kidney stones.

- Salicylates are naturally occurring substances present in raspberries and other fruits. Some people may be sensitive to them. Symptoms like headaches, skin rashes, or congestion in the nose might be brought on by sensitivity to salicylates.

It is important to speak with a healthcare professional or a trained dietitian if you are unsure about ingesting raspberries or if you have any negative responses after doing so. You may still get the health advantages of raspberries while reducing the possibility of possible adverse effects by eating a varied and moderate diet.

Useful parts

Because of their versatility, raspberries may be utilized to prepare a variety of dishes using different parts of the plant. The following are some of the raspberry plant's beneficial parts:

1. Fruit: The fruit of the raspberry plant is, naturally, the portion that people eat the most. You can eat raspberries raw, frozen, or in a lot of different recipes, including smoothies, jellies, jams, and desserts.

2. Leaves: Due to their possible health advantages, raspberry leaves have been used in traditional medicine for generations. They are often dried and steeped to make herbal teas with supposed therapeutic benefits, such as promoting the health of expectant and laboring mothers.

3. Stems and Canes: The tall, prickly stems of the raspberry plant that bear fruit are known as raspberry canes. Raspberry canes are essential for the development and production of the fruit, even though they are not usually eaten. They are also used in agricultural and gardening techniques for cultivation and propagation.

4. Roots: The growth and development of raspberry plants depend heavily on their roots. They serve as the plant's anchor in the ground and take up nutrients and water from the earth. Because raspberry root extract may have therapeutic benefits, it is used in several traditional herbal remedies.

5. Seeds: The tiny, delicious raspberry seeds give the fruit a gritty feel. They are also an excellent source of healthy fats and dietary fiber. For their nutritional value, some individuals decide to eat raspberry seeds, while others like to utilize them in baking and cooking.

6. Flowers: Before the fruit ripens, raspberry flowers are lovely white or pink flowers. Although they are not usually eaten, they are essential to the pollination process because they attract bees and other pollinators, which help to guarantee the production of fruit.

Every component of the raspberry plant has a distinct function and supports the overall development, propagation, and possible applications of the plant. Raspberry advantages extend from the root to the fruit, and they may be savored for their wonderful fruit, added to herbal drinks, or used in gardening techniques.

Chemical constituents

Numerous chemical constituents found in raspberries add to their nutritive value and possible health advantages. The following are some important chemical constituents of raspberries:

1. Antioxidants: Anthocyanins, vitamin C, quercetin, and ellagic acid are just a few of the antioxidant-rich foods that raspberries contain. These substances may lower the chance of developing chronic illnesses and assist in shielding cells from harm brought on by free radicals.

2. Dietary Fiber: Pectin, a soluble fiber, and cellulose, an insoluble fiber, are both found in strawberries. Intestinal health, blood sugar regulation, and weight control all benefit from dietary fiber.

3. **Vitamins:** Vitamins C, K, and E are among the many vitamins that strawberries are an excellent source of. Vitamin K is important for blood clotting and bone health, whereas vitamin C is necessary for collagen synthesis and immune system function.

4. **Minerals:** Manganese, copper, and potassium are among the minerals found in raspberries. Potassium aids in blood pressure regulation and fluid balance, copper is involved in energy generation and antioxidant defense, and manganese is crucial for bone health and metabolism.

5. **Ellagannins:** Ellagannins are polyphenolic chemicals with anti-inflammatory and antioxidant qualities. Raspberries are a good source of these molecules. The body transforms ellagic acid from ellagannins, which can offer a number of health advantages.

6. Flavonoids: Quercetin and kaempferol, two flavonoids found in raspberries, have anti-inflammatory and antioxidant properties. Flavonoids have been linked to a lower chance of developing chronic illnesses, including cancer and heart disease.

7. Anthocyanins: Anthocyanins are a class of flavonoid with antioxidant qualities that give raspberries their rich red color. Anthocyanins could provide some defense against inflammation and oxidative damage.

8. Organic Acids: Malic, citric, and ellagic acids are among the organic acids found in raspberries. In addition to giving the fruit its sour taste, these acids can improve metabolism and digestion.

Together, these chemical constituents give raspberries their distinct taste, color, and even health advantages. Raspberries are a tasty way to increase your intake of important minerals and antioxidants in your diet.

CHAPTER TWO

Varieties, Along With Information On Their Habitat And Cultivation Methods.

Raspberries are a broad category of fruits with several kinds that vary in taste, color, size, and growth patterns. The following list of popular raspberry cultivars includes information about their traits, ideal growing environment, and cultivation methods:

1. Red raspberry:

Characteristics: The most popular kind of raspberries is red ones, which are distinguished by their vivid red color and sweet-tart taste. When harvested, they usually have a hollow center.

Habitat: Red raspberries like plenty of sunshine and well-drained soil. Temperate regions with mild summers and chilly winters are ideal for them.

Cultivation: Red raspberries are usually grown as semi-erect or upright bushes that need supports or trellises to support them. They can be multiplied by root division or stem cuttings, and frequent pruning will ensure maximum fruit output.

2. Black raspberry:

Characteristics: Deep purple-black in color, black raspberries have an earthy, sweet taste. When chosen, they have a central core.

Habitat: Black raspberries thrive best in full sun and well-drained soil, much like red raspberries. They can withstand harsher winter weather.

Cultivation: Black raspberries are usually cultivated as trailing plants, meaning that their canes need to be supported. Pruning is recommended to promote new growth and fruiting since they are propagated by root suckers.

3. Purple raspberry:

Characteristics: The tastes of red and black raspberries are combined to create a hybrid known as purple raspberries. Their flavor is tangy and sweet, and their hue is reddish-purple.

Habitat: Purple raspberries need full light and well-drained soil, just as red and black raspberries do, to thrive.

Cultivation: Trellising is beneficial for purple raspberries, which are usually grown as semi-erect bushes. Stem cuttings are used for propagation, and pruning is necessary to preserve plant health and fruit output.

4. Yellow Raspberry:

Characteristics: Yellow raspberries are valued for their golden-yellow hue and have a softer taste than red or black raspberries. They are often less acidic and sweeter.

Habitat: Yellow raspberries need full light and well-drained soil, just as red raspberries do.

Cultivation: To preserve plant vigor and fruit production, yellow raspberries need to be pruned on a regular basis and supported for their canes, much like red raspberries.

5. Fall Harvest Bliss Raspberry:

Characteristics: Late-season Autumn Bluss raspberries are prized for their luscious, sweet fruit. Their acidity and sweetness are well-balanced.

Habitat: Autumn Bliss raspberries like full sun and well-drained soil. Although they may survive in a variety of conditions, temperate settings are ideal for them.

Cultivation: When grown as bushes, Autumn Bliss raspberries are usually semi-erect or upright and may need assistance. After harvest, trim down the older canes to create space for the new growth since they bear fruit on second-year canes.

8. Cascade Delightful Raspberry:

Characteristics: A more recent type of raspberries called Cascade Delight is prized for its big, tasty berries that have a nice harmony between sharpness and sweetness. They withstand sickness well.

Habitat: Cascade Delight raspberries need steady precipitation and well-drained soil. They can withstand moderate shade, but they thrive in direct sunlight.

Cultivation: Usually cultivated as upright or semi-erect bushes, Cascade Delight raspberries may need assistance. After harvest, trim down the old canes to promote fresh growth and fruiting, since they bear fruit on second-year canes.

Every raspberry variety has special characteristics and needs for cultivation on its own. You can enjoy a plentiful crop of delectable raspberries in your garden by choosing kinds that are suitable for your environment and growth circumstances, giving them the care and maintenance they need, and using the best methods for cultivation.

Propagation

Numerous techniques, including division, tissue culture, root cuttings, and tip stacking, can be used to propagate raspberries. Here are a few popular ways to propagate raspberries:

1.Division:

Method: To make new plants, division entails cutting existing raspberry plants into smaller portions that have roots.

Process: Take out a mature raspberry plant and gently split the root mass into portions, ensuring that the shoots and roots in each division are strong. Prepare the soil, replant the divisions, and give them plenty of water.

Timing: Plants are usually divided in late autumn, after they have gone dormant, or early spring, before new growth starts.

2. Cuts from Roots:

Method: To propagate raspberry roots into new plants, portions of the roots are taken and allowed to grow.

Process: Cut the robust roots of established raspberry bushes into portions measuring 4-6 inches. Plant the root cuttings horizontally, with the top end just below the soil's surface, in a container or straight into the ground. As you wait for new shoots to sprout, keep the soil wet.

Timing: When the plants are still dormant, in late winter or early spring, root cuttings are often collected.

3. Strategy Layering:

Method: To separate a young raspberry cane from its parent plant, bend it to the ground and encourage it to root. This is known as tip-stacking.

Process: Choose a young, flexible cane that is healthy and free of fruiting buds. Bend the cane's tip to the ground, then cover it with earth so that just the exposed portion is visible. Regularly water the layered tip until roots appear. After it has taken root, cut the young plant off of the parent and move it to a different spot.

Timing: When the canes are still pliable and actively developing, early spring is the best time to layer them.

4. Tissue Culture:

Method: Using plant tissue samples, raspberry plants are propagated in a lab environment using tissue culture.

Process: To promote development, small portions of raspberry plant tissue, such as shoot tips or leaf fragments, are sterilized and put in a medium rich in nutrients. Plantlets are created from the tissue samples, and these can be planted in soil to continue growing.

Timing: Mass multiplication of raspberry plants in controlled conditions is a common application for tissue culture, which may be carried out at any time of the year.

Through propagation, gardeners can boost the size of their raspberry patch, swap out unhealthy or old plants, and try out new cultivars. You can effectively grow raspberries and have a flourishing raspberry garden by selecting the appropriate propagation method and adhering to the correct procedures.

Climate and soil needs

Raspberries need a certain kind of soil and temperature in order to flourish and provide an abundant crop. When growing raspberries, keep the following climatic and soil factors in mind:

1. Climate Conditions:

Temperature: Moderate temperatures and temperate climates are preferred by raspberries. In order to prevent cold damage to the canes, they grow best in areas where winter temperatures do not go below -20°F (-29°C) to -10°F (-23°C).

Chill Hours: In order to break dormancy and develop fruit effectively, certain raspberry cultivars need a specific amount of chill hours (hours of cold temperatures) throughout the winter. Verify the chill hour requirements for the particular type of raspberries you are cultivating.

Sunlight: To provide an abundance of fruit, raspberries need full sun. Plant them where they will get at least 6 to 8 hours of direct sunshine each day.

2. Soil Requirements:

Well-Drained Soil: To avoid water-logging, which can cause root rot, raspberries require well-drained soil. Raspberries grow well in soil that is well-drained, either sandy or loamy.

pH Level: Soils between 5.5 and 6.5 are ideal for strawberries; they are slightly acidic to neutral. Find out your soil's pH by doing a soil test, and then make any required amendments.

Organic Matter: Compost or well-rotted manure is examples of organic matter that may be added to the soil to enhance its structure, fertility, and capacity to hold onto water for raspberry plants.

Moisture: Although raspberries like soil with good drainage, they also need steady moisture, particularly throughout the growth and fruiting seasons. Mulching may aid in controlling temperature and preserving soil moisture.

3. Preparing the Soil and Climate:

Prepare the soil by adding organic matter and loosening it to a depth of around 12 to 18 inches before planting raspberries. To lower the danger of illness, choose a planting location with adequate air circulation.

Choose a spot for your raspberry bushes that reduces the hazards associated with the microclimate of your garden, such as windy or frosty patches.

An ideal growth environment for robust plants and an abundant raspberry crop can be established by creating the ideal climate and preparing soil for raspberries. Keeping an eye on the weather, soil moisture, and plant condition throughout the growth season can help you keep your raspberry plants fruitful.

The right planting season

The environment in your area and the propagation technique you choose will determine the best time of year to grow raspberries. Depending on the propagation strategy, the following basic rules apply to the ideal planting season:

1. Transplanting Raspberries Grown in Containers or from Bare Roots:

Spring: It's best to plant bare-root or container-grown raspberry plants in the spring, after your region's last frost date. As a result, the plants are able to take root and develop throughout the growing season.

Fall: Fall planting can additionally be effective in areas with mild winters. If you want to allow your raspberries time to develop before winter dormancy, plant them in the autumn, a few weeks before the first frost.

2. Root Division:

Early spring: The ideal time to split and replant raspberry roots is in the early spring, just before new growth starts, if you're propagating raspberries that way. This facilitates the establishment and growth of the split plants in the next growing season.

3. Cuts from Roots:

Late winter to Early Spring: When the plants are still dormant, this is the best time to take root cuttings for propagation. Now is the time to plant the root cuttings so that they can develop roots and branches when the weather warms.

4. Strategy Layering:

Early spring: When the canes are still pliable and actively developing, tip layering is often done in the early spring. To give the layered tips time to root and develop before the summer growth season, plant them early in the spring.

5. Tissue Culture:

Any Time of the Year: In a controlled setting, like a laboratory, tissue culture propagation can be carried out at any time of the year. The tissue samples can be planted in soil to continue growing when they mature into plantlets.

The optimal time to grow raspberries depends on your local environment and the date of the first frost. When raspberries are planted at the proper time, they have the best chance of developing strong roots, growing quickly, and producing an abundant crop.

To encourage the development of your raspberry plants, make sure you give them the right attention and upkeep during the growing season.

Planting techniques, depths, and spacing

For raspberries to grow and produce well, proper planting is essential. Here are the planting instructions for raspberries, along with planting depth and spacing guidelines:

Steps for Planting:

1. Site Selection: When planting raspberries, choose a sunny spot with well-drained soil.

Steer clear of water-logging zones and regions where raspberries have previously been planted to avoid the spread of disease.

2. Prepare the soil: Till the soil to a depth of 12 to 18 inches; add well-rotted manure, compost, or other organic materials. Test the soil to find its pH level, and if necessary, amend it to get the pH up to 5.5 or 6.5.

3. *Planting:* Create a hole that is big enough to fit the raspberry plant's root system. For plants with bare roots, spread the roots out in the hole and cover them with dirt, pressing the soil firmly yet gently. For plants that were grown in containers, carefully take the plant out of the container, untighten the roots, and plant it in the hole at the same depth as before.

4. *Watering and Mulching:* Make sure the soil surrounding the roots of the just-planted raspberry is settled by giving it a good irrigation.

Cover the plants with an organic mulch layer to keep the soil wet and keep weeds at bay.

Spacing and Planting Depths:

1. Planting Depths:

For bare-root plants, put raspberries at the same depth as they were growing in the nursery container, or at the point where the roots meet the stem.

Steer clear of planting raspberries too deeply, as this could cause the top to rot.

2. Spacing:

Between Rows: To provide simple maintenance access and ventilation, space raspberry plant rows 8 to 10 feet apart.

Between Plants: To allow for growth and spread, place individual raspberry plants two to three feet apart inside the row.

For Trellised Plants: After installing a trellis system, place your raspberries two to three feet apart.

3. Trellising:

Install an elevated structure to support the raspberry canes, and keep them off the ground if you are planting trailing varieties.

As the canes develop, train them along the trellis to provide simpler harvesting and greater air circulation.

These planting instructions, together with recommendations for planting depths and spacing, will help you develop robust raspberry plants that will bear fruit in the future. Pruning, watering, and fertilizing your raspberry bushes on a regular basis can encourage rapid growth and tasty fruit.

Methods for preserving and storing

In order to prolong the shelf life of harvested raspberries and continue to enjoy their delectable taste long beyond the growing season, proper storing and preservation measures are important. Here are a few ways to preserve and store raspberries:

Transient Storage:

1. Refrigeration: Arrange fresh raspberries in a single layer on a tray or container coated with paper towels.

For up to three to five days, keep them refrigerated, ideally in the crisper drawer. In order to avoid moisture accumulation and the formation of mold, wait to wash raspberries until you are ready to use them.

Long-Term Preservation:

1. Freezing: Use a paper towel to gently pat dry the raspberries after giving them a wash in cold water.

Arrange the raspberries on a baking sheet in a single layer, then freeze until solid. Empty the extra air from the frozen raspberries and seal the bag or container that is safe to be kept in the freezer.

You can make use of frozen raspberries in sauces, smoothies, and desserts for up to six to twelve months after they are placed in the freezer.

Conservation:

1. Jam or Jelly: Cook raspberries with sugar and pectin until thickened to make raspberry jam or jelly.

To preserve the jam or jelly for a long time, place it in sterile jars and treat it in a water bath canner.

You can have homemade raspberry jam over toast, pastries, or as an ice cream or yogurt topping.

2. Freeze-Drying: This method prolongs the shelf life of raspberries while preserving their taste and texture.

To freeze-dry raspberries for long-term preservation, use a professional freeze-drying service or a freeze-dryer at home.

Before using freeze-dried raspberries in recipes, rehydrate them by soaking them in water.

3. Dehydrating: Dry and slightly chew raspberries by placing them in a low-temperature food dehydrator or oven.

For many months, keep the dried raspberries in an airtight jar in a cold, dark spot. You can consume dried raspberries as a snack or add them to baked products, trail mix, and granola.

You can maximize your yield and enjoy the flavor of fresh raspberries all year by following these storing and preservation techniques. Try a variety of preservation methods until you discover ones that work best for you and provide you with other ways to enjoy raspberries.

CHAPTER THREE

Weed Control

When growing raspberries, weed management is very important to the health and yield of the plants. Raspberries face competition from weeds for sunshine, water, and nutrients, which may stunt their development and lower their fruit supply. The following are a few successful weed-control strategies for raspberry plants:

1. Mulching:

Surround the base of raspberry plants with a layer of organic mulch, such as wood chips, straw, or crushed leaves.

Mulch preserves soil moisture, controls soil temperature, and releases nutrients as it breaks down. It also helps deter weed development by obstructing sunlight and preventing weed seeds from sprouting.

2. Hand Weeding:

Check the raspberry bed often and pluck weeds by hand, particularly if they are small and simple to remove.

When pulling weeds, take care not to damage the raspberry plants by upsetting their roots.

3. Cultivation:

Gently till the soil around raspberry bushes with a hoe or cultivator to pull out weeds. During cultivation, take care not to harm the raspberry plants' tiny roots.

4. Weed Barrier Cloth:

To stop weeds from growing around raspberry plants, install landscaping cloth or weed barrier fabric.

Make holes in the cloth to fit the raspberry plants, and then tuck the edges in to stop weeds from creeping in.

5. Herbicides:

Only use herbicides as a last option and in the event that cultural and manual weed management techniques prove to be unsuccessful.

Choose an herbicide that is specifically designated for raspberry usage, and carefully follow the manufacturer's recommendations. Take care not to harm raspberry plants by applying herbicides close to them.

6. Cover crops:

To prevent weed development, plant cover crops in between raspberry rows, such as buckwheat or clover.

Cover crops suppress erosion, enhance soil health, and drive out weeds in the race for available nutrients.

7. Regular Maintenance:

To prevent weeds from growing and spreading, keep the raspberry bed well-maintained by mulching, pulling weeds, and cultivating on a regular basis.

Keep an eye out for indications of weed competition on the raspberry plants and act quickly to suppress weeds.

You can encourage healthy development, optimize fruit production, and take pleasure in a bountiful raspberry harvest by putting these weed control techniques into practice and keeping the area around your raspberry plants free of weeds.

Maintaining regular weed control guarantees that the plants get the nutrients they need to grow and is essential to the success of raspberry farming.

How To Control Pests And Diseases

Raspberry plants are susceptible to pests and illnesses that may stunt their development and reduce the amount of fruit they produce. The following are typical pests and illnesses that may harm raspberries, along with practical solutions:

Pests:

1. *Japanese Beetles:* Gather the insects by hand, and then place them in a pail of water with soap. Cover plants with row covers when insect activity is at its highest. Use insecticidal soap or neem oil as a natural pest control measure.

2. Spider Mites: To get rid of spider mites, give plants a powerful stream of water. Use neem oil or insecticidal soap to eradicate spider mite infestations. Use ladybugs or predatory mites as biological control agents.

3. Raspberry Crown Borer: Keep an eye out for any wilting or dieback in the plants. Cut down and eliminate infected canes. Use pesticides that are designated for controlling raspberry crown borer.

Diseases:

1. Powdery Mildew: Proper plant spacing will increase air circulation. Eliminate and discard any diseased plant material. Use fungicides, such as potassium bicarbonate or sulfur.

2. Botrytis Fruit Rot: To avoid infection, harvest ripe fruits as soon as possible. Take out and dispose of contaminated berries. Use fungicides that are labeled to prevent botrytis.

3. Anthracnose: Cut off and eliminate any affected canes by pruning. Use fungicides that include sulfur or copper. To avoid anthracnose, plant resistant cultivars.

4. Root Rot (Phytophthora): To avoid wet circumstances, improve soil drainage. Don't plant raspberries where there is inadequate drainage. Use fungicides with metalaxyl in them to treat root rot.

Strategies for Integrated Pest Management (IPM):

1. Observe: Observe raspberry bushes often for indications of pests and illnesses.

2. Cultural Practices: Keep plants spaced appropriately, feed them enough, and maintain excellent hygiene.

3. Biological Control: Utilize organisms or beneficial insects to manage pest populations.

4. Mechanical Control: Employ physical barriers, trim diseased plant portions, and remove pests by hand.

5. Chemical Control: Take caution while using pesticides and adhere to label directions.

By putting these pest and disease control techniques into practice, you can shield your raspberry plants from frequent dangers, keep them vigorous and healthy, and guarantee a good crop.

Effective management of pests and diseases in raspberry agriculture requires frequent monitoring, early discovery, and timely response.

Chemical Fertilizers, Irrigation Techniques, And Fertilizing.

Fertilization and irrigation are essential components of raspberry plant maintenance for optimum fruit yield and healthy development. The following are recommendations for fertilization and irrigation techniques, including the use of chemical fertilizers:

Irrigation:

Watering Regularly: Raspberries need regular watering, particularly in the growth season and while the fruit is developing. Water sparingly and deeply to promote the development of deep roots.

Apply 1-2 inches of water every week, varying according to the climate.

2. Irrigation Techniques: Soaker hoses or drip irrigation is effective ways to provide water straight to the root zone.

Steer clear of overhead irrigation to keep leaves dry and lower the chance of fungal illnesses.

3. Monitoring Soil Moisture: Use a moisture meter or stick your finger into the soil to check the moisture content of the soil on a regular basis. When the top inch of soil seems dry to the touch, water it.

4. Mulching: To help preserve soil moisture and reduce water evaporation, mulch raspberry bushes with an organic layer. Mulch also enhances soil structure and inhibits weed growth.

Fertilization:

1. Soil Testing: Perform a soil test to ascertain the pH and nutrient content of the soil.

Soil tests are used to determine nutrient deficits and to direct the use of fertilizer.

2. When to Fertilize: Apply fertilizer early in the spring, before the onset of new growth. To avoid too much vegetative growth during fruiting, do not fertilize.

3. Types of Fertilizers: Chemical fertilizers are often utilized to provide raspberry bushes with the vital nutrients they need.

Select a balanced fertilizer, such as a 10-10-10 formulation, that has a nutrient ratio that is appropriate for raspberries.

4. Application rates: Ascertain the appropriate application rate for your raspberry plants by consulting their size and age, and then according to the manufacturer's recommendations.

Distribute fertilizer equally across the plants' drip line, avoiding getting any in touch with the stems.

5. Fertilizer Schedule: Apply fertilizer numerous times throughout the growth season to meet the entire yearly need. Keep an eye on plant development and modify fertilizer application in response to plant needs.

6. Organic Alternatives: Raspberry plants may also be nourished with fish emulsion, compost, or manure, which are examples of organic fertilizers.

Over time, organic fertilizers strengthen soil health by gradually releasing nutrients.

Your raspberry plants will grow healthily, provide a bumper crop, and have general vitality if you employ these watering and fertilizing techniques, along with the use of chemical fertilizers as required.

For best results, keep an eye on the health of your plants, modify fertilizer and watering according to their requirements, and keep a balanced supply of nutrients available.

Methods For Pruning

Maintaining healthy and fruitful raspberry plants requires regular pruning. Fruit quality, air circulation, and sunshine penetration are all enhanced by proper pruning. The following are some of the finest raspberry pruning methods:

1. Summer-Bearing Raspberries:

Annual Pruning: Cut off any fruiting canes after harvest, which is usually in late summer or early autumn.

Thinning: To improve airflow and light penetration, thin out any weak, broken, or crowded canes.

Spacing: To encourage healthy development, leave 4-6 inches between the remaining canes.

2. Fall-bearing (ever-bearing) raspberries:

Two-Part Pruning: Fruit can be produced on both primocanes, or first-year canes, and floricanes, or second-year canes, by ever-bearing raspberries.

Spring Pruning: To promote the development of new primocane, trim down all canes to ground level in the early spring.

Summer Pruning: To create way for fresh growth, cut down the fruited floricanes to the ground after the autumn harvest.

Pruning Steps:

Tools: To ensure accurate cutting without causing damage to the canes, use clean, sharp pruning shears or loppers.

2. *Timing:* Before new growth starts, prune raspberries in late winter or early spring, when they are dormant.

3. *Identify Canes:* First-year, green canes are called primocanes and are often thinner and more flexible.

4. Cutting Technique

Summer-Bearing: trim out remaining canes as required and cut fruited canes at ground level.

Everbearing: For primocanes and floricanes, use the two-part pruning technique.

5. Remove Weak Growth: To promote stronger growth, prune off weak, spindly canes.

6. Clean Up: To lessen disease pressure and preserve cleanliness, remove trimmed canes from the planting area.

7. Training: To keep the remaining canes erect and arranged, tie them to a trellis or other support structure.

Additional Methods:

Renovation Pruning: To revitalize overgrown or neglected raspberry patches, think about renovation pruning, which involves cutting all canes to the ground in late winter.

Sanitation: To stop plant diseases from spreading, clean and sanitize pruning instruments on a regular basis.

Observation: Throughout the season, keep an eye on the development and health of your raspberry plants and make any necessary modifications.

By adhering to these optimal pruning methods for raspberries and customizing them to your particular variety, you may encourage robust development, optimize fruit yield, and preserve the general well-being of your raspberry plants. Pruning on a regular basis is essential to long-term raspberry-growing success and a plentiful yield.

Harvesting And Handling After Harvesting

In order to guarantee the quality and shelf life of raspberries, harvesting and post-harvest management are essential procedures. The following are some tips for harvesting and managing raspberries:

Harvesting:

1. Time: Pick raspberries when they are completely ripe yet still firm. A little pull can readily remove ripe raspberries from the plant.

2. Frequency: Because raspberries ripen fast, check raspberry flowers often throughout the busiest time of year. Pick ripe berries every two to three days to avoid spoiling or over ripening.

3. Handling: Take care while handling raspberries to prevent injury and bruises. Gently grasp the fruit with your thumb and fingers, then twist it to remove the stem.

4. Storage: To avoid crushing and promote air circulation, store gathered raspberries in shallow containers. To keep raspberries fresh, keep them refrigerated between 32 and 34°F (0 and 1°C).

Handling After Harvest:

1. Sorting: Sort raspberries to get rid of any berries that are rotten, overripe, or damaged. To avoid contamination, throw away any berries that exhibit indications of deterioration.

2. Cleaning: Right before eating, give raspberries a gentle rinse under cool running water. Steer clear of soaking raspberries, as they may absorb moisture and get mushy.

3. Drying: Before storing, pat dry raspberries with a paper towel or clean cloth to absorb any remaining moisture. Sufficient moisture may shorten shelf life and encourage the formation of mold.

4. Packaging: To promote ventilation, place raspberries in breathable containers or perforated plastic bags. Steer clear of too tightly packed raspberries, as this may result in bruising and spoilage.

5. Transportation: Take extra care while handling raspberries to avoid damage. To preserve quality, keep raspberries chilled while in transportation.

6. Storage: For optimal quality, keep raspberries refrigerated and use them within a few days.

In addition, strawberries can be frozen for extended periods of time by first arranging them in a single layer on a baking sheet and then moving them to a freezer bag.

These harvesting and post-harvest management procedures will help you keep your raspberries tasty, fresh, and of the highest quality. Because raspberries are sensitive, treatment throughout the harvest and storage phases is essential to maintaining their quality and extending their shelf life.

How To Promote And Make Sales From Raspberry Farming.

Here are some tactics to think about when it comes to promoting and selling raspberries:

1. Identify Your Target Market: Choose your target audience, which may include local customers, food processors, farmers' markets, grocery shops, and restaurants.

2. Branding: Create a compelling brand identity for your raspberries by emphasizing their quality and freshness via your packaging, logo, and message.

3. Online Presence: Establish a website or online shop to highlight your raspberries and provide details about your farm or business. Make use of social media channels to interact with consumers, offer information, and advertise your products.

4. Local Markets: You may sell your raspberries to customers directly by taking part in farmers' markets, roadside stalls, or community gatherings.

Establish connections with nearby merchants, eateries, and chefs to provide them with fresh raspberries.

5. Community Engagement: To inform the community about your raspberries and farming methods, host farm tours, seminars, or tasting events. Work together to find chances for cross-promotion with other nearby manufacturers or companies.

6. Quality Assurance: To earn clients' confidence, make sure your raspberries are of the highest caliber, fresh, and defect-free.

To appeal to ecologically aware customers, think about getting certifications such as organic or sustainable agricultural techniques.

7. Customer Service: Offer first-rate customer service, which includes quick answers to questions, adaptable payment plans, and easy ways to have things delivered or picked up. Request client comments and evaluations to enhance your goods and services.

8. Promotions and Discounts: To draw in new business and keep hold of current clientele, provide promotions, discounts, or loyalty programs. Make unique or seasonal packages to promote higher sales.

9. Packaging and Presentation: Give your raspberries aesthetically pleasing and useful packaging that both preserves and highlights the fruit's beauty. Think of enhancing the value by including recipe cards, gift baskets, or educational resources.

10. Review and Adjustment: Get input from clients on their likes, recommendations, and general contentment with your raspberries.

To remain competitive, make constant adjustments to your marketing plans based on feedback from customers and industry changes.

You can reach a larger audience, boost sales, and successfully promote your product by putting these marketing and sales methods into practice. Creating a strong brand, interacting with consumers, and providing top-notch goods are essential components of a profitable raspberry marketing and sales strategy.

Printed in Great Britain
by Amazon